DIVIDED TONGUES

Patrick Davidson Roberts was born in 1987 and grew up in Sunderland and Durham. He was editor of *The Next Review* magazine 2013-2017, co-founded Offord Road Books press in 2017 and reviews for The Poetry School and The High Window. His debut collection is *The Mains* (Vanguard Editions, 2018), and a chapbook, *The Trick* (Broken Sleep Books, 2023), was recently published. His poetry has elsewhere been published in *14 Magazine, Acumen, Ambit, The Dark Horse, Eyot, The Interpreter's House, Long Poem Magazine, Magma, The Quince, The Rialto,* and on *Atrium, Bad Lilies, The High Window, One Hand Clapping* and *Wild Court*, as well as in anthologies published by Culture Matters, New River Press, Sidekick Books and Vanguard Editions.

I was born on both sides of the border, between
agreement and crossed fingers.

The part of the land that was passed to the Northman
holds hard in the vowels, while

that warmer stretch of sea to sea
governs the uglier parts of my tongue.

Between agreement and crossed fingers, then,
was that thing in me made which,

renegade or liar, cannot
craft a sentence without crossing

the line long agreed to mark off the
abandoned from the hoarded.

Endgame being confrontation, you wonder
deals are made at all. I step over the Danelaw's

border each time I say something longer
than a single word from either side.

Also by Patrick Davidson Roberts

The Trick (Broken Sleep Books, 2023)

The Mains (Vanguard Editions, 2018)

CONTENTS

SOMETHING TO DO WITH DOGS	13
THE TITANIC	14
DIVIDED TONGUES	16

    PETER
    JAMES THE GREAT
    ANDREW
    BARTHOLOMEW
    JUDE THADDEUS
    SIMON THE ZEALOT
    JAMES THE LESS
    MATTHEW
    JUDAS
    MATTHIAS
    THOMAS
    PHILIP
    PAUL
    JOHN

THE ORAL FIX	30
ADMIRALTY ARCH	32
THE RIG	33
HYPATIA OF ALEXANDRIA	36
THE OFFER	38
THE GREEN KNIGHT	39
THE TRAIN	40

    FIRST BROADCAST RECEIVED
    SMOKE IN THE MORNING
    THE WAR MEMORIAL
    THE LYCHGATE
    STRUGGLE
    THE TRAIN

THAT NO PRISON WILL HOLD YOU	46
THE CANON	47
LILBURNE'S PRAYER	49
JESUS AMONG THE SCORPIONS	50
BACK OFF AGAIN	51
SEPTEMBER AND OCTOBER	52

TWO NATIVITIES 2023
    FROM MATTHEW
    FROM LUKE
	55

HALFWAY FROM HELL TONIGHT	57
PETER THE HERMIT	58
FINAL SUMMIT ATTEMPT	59
THE HELL AND HIGH	64
THE GUILTY	65
MISTER HANDTOTHROAT	67
APHRODITE	69
SPEECH	70
STRAIGHTSMOUTH	71
ACKNOWLEDGMENTS	75

For Mam and Dad

© 2025, Patrick Davidson Roberts. All rights reserved. No part of this book may be reproduced, stored in a retrieval system, or transmitted in any form or by any means, whether electronic, mechanical, photocopying, recording, or otherwise, without the prior written permission of the publisher, except in the case of brief quotations used in reviews or scholarly works.

This work may not be used for text and data mining, including (without limitation) the training of artificial intelligence technologies or systems. The author and publisher expressly reserve all rights and opt out of any applicable text and data mining exceptions.

ISBN: 978-1-917617-49-9

Cover designed by Aaron Kent

Edited and Typeset by Aaron Kent

The author has asserted their right to be identified as the author of this Work in accordance with the Copyright, Designs and Patents Act 1988

Broken Sleep Books Ltd
PO BOX 102
Llandysul
SA44 9BG

Divided Tongues

Patrick Davidson Roberts

Broken Sleep Books

These people are not drunk, as you suppose. It's only nine in the morning.
— Acts 2:15

In other words, let's confine ourselves to the other words.
— *Otherwise Engaged*, Simon Gray

But remember that words are signals, counters. They are not immortal. And it can happen - to use an image you'll understand - it can happen that a civilisation can be imprisoned in a linguistic contour which no longer matches the landscape of... fact.
— *Translations*, Brian Friel

SOMETHING TO DO WITH DOGS

Dropping low, off the end of the ridge, I finally caught
the keys in my pocket which had been smacking me all the way down
and grappled their star in the teeming red of my cold right palm.
I leant against the other side of the first wall that I found and tried
to shake myself into shape. The winter had blown me past burden,
from the summit and spine and now to the valley.
The Half Moon only a slope away, I ground myself down to the lip of it when,
out of a wailing mop of thicket, he pushed himself along to me,
rain whipping from his hood, and the beard beneath like rag.
'This has been a while coming!' he shouted over the gale
and gripped my shoulder to steady before 'But we have to go back up.'
I gripped the keys tight in my fist and shook what was left of my head.
He spat at me something to do with dogs and started the climb again.
I looked to where I'd come from, and to where he went,
but the scale of the storm was now past my ken,
with him gone to it in a matter of minutes.
Once I'd lost him, I headed down, got through the door, dropped my bag
and burst into prayers at the bar. Later, the lights didn't flicker but failed.

THE TITANIC

Out of history they landed the ship's hulk in the earth: straight up from the ground.
Again it comes down to how many people – and when they say 'people', you know –
they can shut in, when death comes reaching. Steerage, in Kensington.

Consider Captain Smith. There were those around him who said 'He went silent,
can you imagine it? Silent!' Captain Smith who, once on deck, knew that it had been
required that lifeboats be removed – a matter of aesthetics – from the First Class promenade.

Smith, who knew the popular chorus: 'Every ship should be her own lifeboat', which
over a century later still reads as 'Just stay put'. Take a further drink. Go back inside,
for the cold outside is dangerous. Stay where you are. They are coming.

Now excuse with ease an absence of effort to move those praying as their kneeling tilts:
Who would deny them their only comfort? What kind of man interrupts prayers?
The purest water came to them, and the waters of ablution always shock the saved.

A Catholic school of thought would still propose, one hundred and five
    years later,
that 'Common sense' should be enough to lead people from the fire, and
    such a school
would read the line between Common sense and Common as applied to
    steerage.

God should be neither questioned nor elbowed away, besides: what life had
    they?
Something about that Commonality, when handed down, apparently dies
in the passage of fire. So much of that Common is engulfed by fire and flame.

We come in from over the Westway into London swerving in and out
of sightlines, and then the Titanic rises up, in Kensington, before our eyes
in lifeboats of another gilt. Burnt, bodied, still fucking there. It silences the
    air around.

DIVIDED TONGUES
for Fran Lock

Peter

As the professional lays you out, with your skull off the edge of the bed,
you cut off your airway rather than face the glass there translating the scene.
At eleven the walk out of town had beckoned, to shrug off the heat of the streets,
and maybe the coast in an hour, once out, but then you bumped into that guy.
He was catching a drink in the usual place; past the station, before the arena,
and didn't you fancy one? It was your turn. You followed and fell in behind,
back to bad habits and company that you had always known to be over your head.
Two drinks in, the professional caught you stretching, and gestured to follow
    them up.
Laid out, you knew things had gone the wrong way, but without the words to
    right them.
They left you crossly; the headache hatching, the payment finally made,
while down in the bar, as they ask where he went – having just twigged the
    guy's face –
he asks himself *Where am I off to?* as you had, though his is no end of escape.
As you drift into pain and to night, the airway gives up and you dream
that you're back on the road, but this time alone; stopping for no man, for
    nothing.

James the Great

Let me tell you about thunder. It breaks when you ask questions:
thunder broke when you were refused the answers and so your eyes bellowed.
Thunder broke when you came home late to find your brother already at his desk
while your mother screamed about wasted years and why she regretted only you.
Thunder was the word about town when the news broke of his
having taken the money raised for the children's school and blown it in Reno.
Thunder was how you spoke to him when you wanted to be gentle
but instead felt your wrists pinned to the wall and burned through that hour.
Thunder sounded the streets around as everyone else ran to hide, but you
heard only your father, and faced it down in the car, in the street.
Thunder was what broke the blood from your gums as they pulled the third tooth,
cut another finger away. Thunder was what you called them
and thunder was how they came. Thunder was the sight of the blade, the bite
of your teeth on the curb. Thunder was the fire you called down. Thunder was
    the world.

Andrew

You'd always wondered where the spot would mark you
and struggled with whether it blessed or condemned.
Shifting the net between your hands at night, mending fireside,
you turned the interweave to horizontal then vertical,
and did often, for luck. That was the way you wanted the world.
Straight up: complementary, *truer*, you thought.
Only when you leant closer to the fire, as the others came in
having turtled the boat for the night, did you realise the diagonal
in your palm. Quickly you'd turn it away from thoughts of *wrong*.
Today awoken in Metaxa sweat, you heard the fishing boats go out
and caught the salt air whipping back from them, to where you stretched yourself.
Another hilltop, more olive trees, no signs of more than either.
The fisherman found you this afternoon, caught against the light:
that tilted cross of yourself, fixed, and the day gone from behind you.

Bartholomew

At the lift-head they pulled you out, then recoiled.
You were handed to the unwanting and finally laid down, you
suddenly a thing of tissue and bleed, new. You
were barely covered, and the blanket barely covered you, above,
and the talk about your body was of the *extreme gas explosion*.
Some few friends, remembering, made their way forward
and as the pit foreman held his cap and spoke of mercies
they took care to peel you back. The fibers stuck
to your glisten, your reply. How fantastic and blazing
must have been that time above ground, far and in the blinding light!
You'd spoken in the showers, canteen, past the slagheap,
of all that moved from dark to light and of what could possibly be imagined.
As the skin of your arm sagged in your own palm, brother, we believed;
gained another among us, before they took you away.

Jude Thaddeus
　i.m. M. Colvin

Crater after crater, you saw reporters scatter

and clocked the weirdness of earth when broken by battle.

Scrambling to the corner, you rehearsed *I am* and *I'm*

in both their languages, each far from a farmer's tongue.

In everything you knew the divide and at this moment too

you saw the hatchet on the ground as a symbol handed to you.

Fragmenting Homs burst around your head. You ran, thrown

so that you landed on the ground in a pattern mappable to man.

Sheltering among the collapse and the building going down,

you clutched the icon to you. Deaf, it was the only sound.

When they dragged you to the square, bloody and done,

you took them to take the axe and make two from one.

Instead you heard the laugh. Clicks. Time's camera.

The club raised, you bowed. Your head stamped out. Maranatha.

Simon the Zealot

Even now the force of feeling is enough to bite you in half.
You have watched her from the town hall steps, watched her make
her bloody way with cries of liberty and death that rang every bell in you.
This country was not built for you, but you find the history of struggle
one and the same with your own. There's something about zeal,
when dealt with at this pitch. She almost brought the day of flame back
to mind: language lessons, the sing of the right words and spit of the new.
Next year you will go back to Urfa, walk the streets of decline and death
with these stories for your payday, but even then it will be as though
men held you down and cut you in two with the sharpest teeth they could find,
such will be the memory of the cries in the marketplaces,
the coming whirl of riot and loot. You could have sworn that she knew you:
read the hiss of revolt in your eyes, last night, and maybe that was why.
But this morning you took a pamphlet and left, torn apart once more.

James the Less

Dear Cousin, sometimes I think that I disappeared into you, as if
the sun was made flesh when you stood at the end of the bed
to ask if I were warm enough. So few mentions I receive, in your letters,
your book tour, your interviews across the sea.
I pick my way through your words as if they will seal me to you
but with the lock on the other side. I am told by doctors that I dreamt everything.
Even now, here, as if to prove them all correct.
I did not dream the feel of you nor the morning as you dressed
beside the bed and I sat to hold your bare thigh for a second, see
the hair fall to your waist and the tracery of a smile dart across your lips.
I must leave for a long time to climb out of such silence, and so
that is why I write now. I will tell everyone about you when I speak again.
I know that they do not believe me; you don't, but for one night I was heard
and even if you lied then I believed you. That was enough. And this.

Matthew

Tel Aviv, and walking past another bar you saw the coding,
saw the loving layers of numbers. They had hated you for those.
You step into the bar, remove the fanboy cap, squint at the dark.
He's In – I'll Follow   You move up to the bar and ask for a password.
They hand you it with the beer. You move to the front, smile, drink.
As you connect you remember that communication was not pain
and that you were sure of that, in his sight.   *I Have A Clear Shot – Request*
  Authorisa-
No. All of those numbers. You've been walking. Outside. Smoke.
You step out of the shop, watch your bag, remove your coat. Breathe.
Negative – Not Clean – I'm Moving Outside   The sunlight tightens
and the air in the arcade grips. 'Fucking things,' you mutter
as you heel it. You are a good man. He told you so. They said that you weren't
but he told you so. Two weeks back you broke the story, on the cabinet minister
fucking her over the dockside. Was it   *Alpha – Yes –*
  Confirmation – Down

Judas

You'd spent the night flat on the strongest branch
as a snake reflecting and hanging its tail like a rope until
some witless stranger wraps the length of it round his body.
Noise in the suburbs, a din in her washing his feet, and his smile.
They turned you down at the meeting; you, and your talk of investment.
She'd laughed at you, too, as he'd ordered you out.
You knew principles to be barely skin-deep among them,
the way that they carried on, decided that now was the time.
But first you stood on the branch, then sat with the dusk,
before the night flat on your stomach, her wet hair and eyes in your head.
Oh all that time you had brimmed with such colourless hate,
until this height beckoned you. Her messages still in your pocket;
that *it's only for show, when he's around*, but then that brimming again.
You fell asleep. That's how she found you. The coins in the blood beneath.

Matthias

What nobody ever mentions is you having to deal with the body.
Two deaths in and they called you, dragged you out of bed with need.
For the first it looked simple – suicide gone wrong – but the second,
staring up at the wood, you couldn't be sure. They whispered promotion.
You had to call Maggie into your office, first day on the job, tell her
that you knew that she was telling people about the voices, the drink, the pills.
She took it well, but with that look, and it didn't make a difference.
You could have told them, and wanted to, that you'd been there at the river
when the first body was brought out; the baptism, so to speak;
so you knew how flesh can change and had seen them all confused. But.
You cut his image from the card and stuck yours there instead.
A year into the case and the lead took you to the bone-merchants, cannibals.
That night you took the knife, went out into that town, and as they turned to
    grip you
remembered that you had dealt with bodies, so could take a place, and let them.

Thomas

On the edge of Madras and about to hand yourself over at last
you scatter the leaflets behind you, and check that you haven't heard from him.
Nothing. Plenty from the rest, though. Some days it's nothing but news.
Each picked up their story, ran with it.
The night is curdling, with the quayside shouting and lit
which beckons you down to the fleshpot closest to the sea.
The fish char on the coals by the bar, but you haven't touched fish in years.
Half a carafe of the darkest red carries you out to the street.
Business is done carefully between those wandering eyes
and more than a single man starts to suggest. Which makes you think of
If you can only believe me like this as you moved inside, wrapped yourself
in the warmth of his hold. Perhaps, at the end of it all, one last touch could do.
'…*my* god,' are the final words that the medic hears
holding your hand as you bleed out, the crowd being told to move back.

Philip

Even headfirst the earth seems far away. Even when dived at.
Not everything can be so inverted. Your words came out the same today,
are forming the right-way-up even now, but something
about you has changed. When you reach up to the earth
you do so in stasis, and hit the street. Your sister cries out
and turns from the window, running to jump the stairs and come down.
Even spraddled on the paving stones, arms outstretched and feet together,
you do not want to go back. Better to finish here, surely.
Remembering now those days of their pleading with you to return
to the group, but you had set out to the work, and like a tanker underway
could only turn slowly, if you turned at all, took a full arc to comply.
She cradles your broken frame in her hands now, her own face bleeding,
and gently presses the raw tattoo of the steel square on your wrist.
'They're going to let me go, now,' *Then, sister, do the same.*

Paul

You were crossing Cambridge Circus, the hour after dawn,
when I saw the man in uniform turn to you at the far side.
He'd been leading you up from the darkness near the centre
and the rising road had grown light past squares and shops alike,
but now he stopped with you exposed, still stood in the road.
He shuffled uncomfortably in his boots and helmet, tightened straps
and hooked one thumb in the wide belt bearing the weapon.
I watched you both, as I wrote this down, from my place in the sun.
He pointed at the space between you, and looking down you saw
the white outline, exact to the second, of all the years behind.
I could not see whether he offered his hand or took yours first
before the traffic took you, and chaos filled the crossroad.
After the uniforms had gone, I walked to the barrier.
Your body had fallen perfectly into the space prepared,
but your thoughts lay beyond this place, as they had done all those years.

John
 C.

Neither dreamed of nor prayed for you were there.
Not with the force of your presence, nor in my sadness.
Four long years and every day a tremor, building from your absence,
for weeks a drink was beyond my grasp and I could only shake.
I'd walk the rain at midnight with a quake close to tearing my arm.
And this was neither prophecy nor the mark of Cain, but instead
the dreadful weight of the love that I have forced down, since.
There you were. Neither dreamed of nor prayed for
but longed for all these years. I am the last who tells.
I expected an island, or a walk across fields.
Instead I had a wet night, and the lights on the ground beneath you,
the brightest above your head. Your face more brilliant than memory
and the long years between then and now blasting to night.
Winds' crash longed for as the end. You were there. I shook.

THE ORAL FIX

Halfway through, or so I hope, I recross my arms and move
my other hand to grip the other wrist. The blood
rushes back, which I hope that she doesn't spot.
She notices something, though, and asks if I'm ok.
Seeing very little point in the radioactive afterlife
of toxic masculinity if I can't use it to lie to someone
about how much they are hurting me,
I nod with my eyes and affect a calm not reflected in the rest of my pose.
In fairness to her, she's not causing anything bad directly.
The pain that is coursing through me, so
like the bad doses of junk that kept me from
the dentist for the time that they did,
is to do with the fact that anyone at all is touching me
when my mouth is open.
Years back, having been driven to make
a dental appointment for the first time in too long
by my mother's comments, I'd done so with the expectation
that, the best part of two decades having been spent
feeding only my worst interests,
pretty much everything was going to be dragged out.
Lying back that time, I'd more or less resigned myself
to wholesale uprooting and committed removal,
and when she started the inspection I'd accepted

the incoming damage ahead. I wouldn't have minded her

touching me, then, as long as it was purely to rip stuff out

and cause me the deep and lingering pain that people like her can do.

As it was, my younger years avoiding – or not being allowed,

which become the same thing – anything sweet and most things sugar

had carried my teeth through later years of neglect.

Even the one filling that I have is to do with

a smack in the mouth in my teens, something that I

have stopped telling people, having realised that fights

aren't as sexy to bring up as I'd spent years assuming.

Now here I am crossed and recrossing myself,

and realising that I may have arrived at

an age where the violence is lessening,

both in me and in those around me, but that

I have become increasingly terrified of people touching me at all,

even when its fix is spitting, and that, no, I am not going to clarify

who is doing what to whom. We passed that point a while back.

ADMIRALTY ARCH

They are taking down the scaffolding around Admiralty Arch. They are pulling down years from around the stonework and uncovering beneath. They are opening up Admiralty Arch as at the opening of ancient tombs, as at the clearing back of a long-buried tunnel trapping the trains inside. A crowd stands back, thronging the Mall, waiting to see what's within. Plank after plank is withdrawn and the walkways peel back and away until nothing is left but Admiralty Arch and the right-hand-side tunnel when you're facing this way that leads beneath to Whitehall. They are excavating Admiralty Arch and I must be the first to glimpse the find so am straining myself past tourist and cordon to stare into that passageway. Nothing. Clear sight. A passage cleared for concourse and conduct. Fuck. Even now I expected to find something like the trapped of Pompeii, to see two people caught in the cloud of each other in that tunnel, pressed against the wall, their dark forms and night, that night, of joy captured; caught as me, though even I must admit I knew that, to look at us now, you'd never know.

THE RIG
Ár kváðu ganga
grœnar brautir
flgan ok aldinn
ás kunnigan,
ramman ok r skvan
Ríg stíganda.
 – Line 1 of *Rigsthula* (The Song of Rig)

You sense him as the breath in the backdraft, the smoke in the slipstream,
or scent in a simmer. His card would call him the black in the ink-stain
and credit his feel as rough in a rockface. Down to town he was more
the man in the crowd than the face in the crowd beside him, for you
could never tell him apart from himself or the dozens that he became.
All this was to simple ends, as the custody suits, the *Have You Seen*s
and the *Missing Persons* will all attest. Then there were the generations
of overlap in telltale and rumour, and the jealousy of mother, of daughter.
Could you tell it was him, though? I mean, are you sure it was him?
I heard he left his coat behind, before setting out to the wrong side of town.

That's what they said a century back, when he first pops up in the chat.
Down at the riverside her mother's gran kept *The Old Mud House*, with her man,
and that's the first we see of the Rig, coming along the waterfront, cocky-like.
It was a quiet day – match going on in another town, and hardly a drinker to see.
They'd kept the stove going, just in case, but with little thought to the use when
    it came.
He kneed the door with apologies, had them pour him one and one for themselves.
Half an hour on and the pot was empty and full, and the bottle nearly done.
They locked themselves away for the night like two bands wrapped round a barrel.
In the morning they awoke to an empty hold, but nine months on changed that.
Wasn't pretty, but strength is usually ugly, and he was useful around the place.

Her grandmother says he was late stopping by, almost last orders at *The Garden Gate*,
while her husband was doing the door and couldn't see such a name on the list.
He'd asked to check, as he should have been there, and by the time that
he'd handed it back, there it was – 'Rig' – though the ink looked wet.
A matter of charm then, him at the bar, as the two of them shut the place up.
A couple of plays on her dimples, her laugh, and she'd handed him another.
By the time the sun woke her husband, they were kissing goodbye out the back.
While they never saw him again, they talked about it more than you'd think.
Her mother swears she's her father's nose and a little of his twitch in her toes
but the rest is down to her husband, which seems a fair enough split.

Now you'll hear folk say that that time *he came back, the child being grown,*
with a mind to take her away, but had second thoughts once he saw her, and didn't.
But that's the shit you get from people who need a reason for why they smacked
that guy last Thursday when they didn't like his look and could
tell he wasn't from round here and not to be going after the women and there are too many
of them come here and would you get the fuck away. Easy to hang the blame for a stranger
on someone alien after time, or someone unusual after a drink – even to hide
from your own sense of waste and the daughter at home and the wife long gone.
No, he didn't come back. Not to her, in any case, though money came once in a while.
They put it away to send her away, for she was meant for beautiful things.

Did you hear her own story, though? Now that's a tale to tell.
Not only herself involved, or so her daughter told me – with a little too much detail
for me to think her herself alright. Same setup, different bar: *The Empty Space*,
about two days on. Then again, her mother was a bit more open-minded
      – her guy too –
them being a bit of the finer stuff, on account of that expensive school, on account
of her alabaster tone and the wheat-streak of blonde to her hair. They
      welcomed him in
having read his plate from afar: RIG, and gave him the full spread, both of them.
With this story, he *does* come back – I should know; he caught us at it.
I haven't seen her in years, no, she's away in the city, with a guy that she met
who was the dead spit of him and all. I heard that he set them up.

But listen to us. You know where it's headed. If the two of them get some
there'll be twelve of them and on and on it goes. But for my money
she's just the one, Conor, and I've seen him about on the heath.
Same as his mother, I mean same weird way to him, talking to birds
and not the right ones. They'd have him a doctor, a fireman, a judge,
I'm sure, but he's his own tale to tell. Each time that I find him talking to ravens
he tells me they're setting him up in the houses of other men,
and that one day the world will be his. And then he just laughs, like the splash
in a downpour, shakes his dark eyes like coal in the night. The look of the tale,
have you met him? He was here just– look, he's left his coat.

HYPATIA OF ALEXANDRIA
For Yvonne Reddick

In my telling, she is standing as she might have chosen on the sand beside
    the sea,
with the tip of her right index finger pressed to her right thumb
and that scope held up to her eye with the stars beyond, contained, within.
And while she knows that so much lies therein that cannot be so simply caught
she is happy that at least as much as she has worked out works,
is there, before her.

In my telling, though she would not have known it, there's a parallel
between what she is doing and what, a small way on, Sigurd would do,
when asked. He held a solar stone up to the dark and was able to locate the sun.
And while, for both, violence was coming, the sky and all its education
was enough for those moments.

In my telling, she turns her lens and narrows an eye and sees raging men,
and the O of her fingers turns bloody and dark, and the sky disappears.
In my telling, she remains on the shore, and the ellipsis that would not kill
    Copernicus,
nor butcher Galileo, is in the imperfect ring that she has made with our fingers.
And if she thinks of the burning library, it is as nothing to this.

In my telling, she has seen the route, and as she leaves the beach

there is only what she alone can assess

and what we have remembered,

that one day will be termed *in a blade of grass,*

though she smiles that now

it is in her hand.

THE OFFER

The meeting began at eleven the approved minutes will read.
She finds this funny, given that comments –
on outcomes, compromise, the deal, that lot –
were already being uncased and balanced in the boardroom
from ten-thirty onwards, though she felt no need
to insist on this point, on signing-off her copy. Not discontent,
then: after all, she'd given her side of it a decent shot.
Fifteen minutes at least, which even they'd not presume
to dismiss completely. She frowned at the minutes.
Fuck's sake – eleven! By then they were almost done with it.

'Nemine contradicente': *with nobody contradicting.*
Nem con, as she'd learned from him seven years ago.
Which was rubbish, even then. If no dissent existed,
why were they facing each other in the first place?
'Mutatis mutandis' was closer to the meaning:
all necessary changes having been made. She should know.
'…your colleague states that at no point were his actions resisted.'
As the figure was agreed she forced herself to stare at his face.
Her new office waited, a full flight up from her last,
as did his smirk, the next time they passed.

THE GREEN KNIGHT

Breaking from the dawn, I started my way south,
taking my world wrapped tight around me.
The grieving glades, west-water shorebirds, wilds.
The fur I wore beneath plate turned rag and stained
in sap from the holly branch gripped before me,
from all my winter, gods of Wirral and wolf alike.

Mere life was my journey down: what of all, man, beast and trunk
that on my way ducked to avoid, or else licked around
the burr of my axe or turn of my shade? Life, mere life.
Oh world. Where are we but here?
Here arrived, armed only with this metal icon of blade
mounted upon this branch, and that now another arm,
its lichen, leaf and stem all matched to this skin.
My blood up, as I enter their story.

THE TRAIN
for Kirsten Irving

First Broadcast Received

You remember that Tuesday night after Jill left, that Tuesday.
It was the first we'd heard the news about the coast, and that
they'd got here, they'd landed, and all bets were off. Weird that we
were in such a good mood, given such a slim week, one town only.

That night we lit the fire properly and there was music, and we broke
the drink out like we'd imagined would only happen at the end of something.
Tariq finally cuddling with Jen, all of the families eating together,
and the watches constant, happy. The valley around safe. Safe.

I had kissed the twins goodnight, and held Cass for an hour.
Stepping out to check the perimeter, I felt Orion's Belt pulse,
wished for more days or nights like this. Lisa took the beer from me,
took my hand. The bracken behind the truck. Cries. The beer on her lips.

Smoke in the morning

After breakfast was done with, and the stamping and straining
of boots began, Thom asked his usual question. I winced.
Lisa took it this time, 'West. Second town over. There by eleven, maybe.
We'll check the farms below the ridge on the way. There might still be stragglers.'

I rolled the tent up, fastened it tight, threw it into the back of the truck.
Then got the twins into their car seats and made that sure Cass had the map.
The motors tuned each other, and Cass nodded *Good luck* through the window.
In five minutes the group of cars were filling the lanes away from us.

I took the left, with Lisa's last cigarettes, and she the far right, a mile off.
The ten of us strung out as the mist, stepping over wire and broken stone
as we picked towards the first of the farms. I mingled smoke with the morning
and was content with my own company. By the time they opened fire I was set.

The War Memorial

An hour later we had reached the marketplace, ears still ringing.
Even holding the scarf to my face, the smell of fire and flesh stung.
Entering from the higher alleys we gingerly picked our way forward,
towards the central crash of debris, the town hall burning beyond.

Thom went back to the supermarket car park, coughing, to tell the others.
I'd asked Jen if stopping there would be secure enough for them,
though Lisa had answered instead 'Yes. Three ways out. Even in a hurry.'
I nodded and raised my arm, waiting, until Thom turned and did the same.

Tariq was moving the smouldering planks aside from the War Memorial,
when Cass came through, 'Can you hear me? We're here. Watch set.'
The sound of the twins jabbering in the background. I walked to the planks
with Jen. Beneath there were four or five. Peeled. Pink. Well done.

The Lychgate

Jen asked me if I was all right, while the others dealt with the Post Office and filled the back seats of the cars. I could hear them bundling the sweating milk cartons into the footwells, wedging half-squeezed sliced loaves beside one another on the seats. Could hear the kids happy with new toys.

The evening was lengthening, or something like that; it was getting dark. I had given the first kick at the door once I thought the town absent. Thom had followed through the caved wood, I don't know if I heard someone inside, but I heard Thom make it all open and quiet.

'I'm fine.' Could feel her eyes at my side. I hissed to the side, half-spit, and she went back to help with the shop. In front of me the lychgate was on fire. Such old wood, screaming its last moments. The church beyond dark, apart from that sudden flash at the window. This time I said nothing.

Struggle

Matilda has grown taller than Stephen. Which is what we all expected.
Jen shoos us all away when Steve starts crying 'My sister is *taller!*'
The grief of a six year-old at just-ten Matilda. Still Jen assures him, louder,
that 'It's all about time, Stephen, wait for the time. You'll be a big boy.'

Cass takes Mattie to the river, with the twins, whenever there's a river to go to,
but understands the distance that this builds. She tries to stop doing it.
As much as I don't know, I've mentioned to Cass that 'It's different for an aunt:
Jen is always going to feel like there's an obvious door that she hasn't opened.'

Last night, once the songs were done, Jen showed us the stilts that she'd made.
I could see Owen smile to his bones, and thanked him for helping. God, the way
that kid looked, having put the gleaming stilts on. Even Mattie laughed, and
  bowed.
Different for an aunt, though, no matter that thing fixed. Soon she'll have to tell
  them.

The Train

The concern, unspoken amongst us, was whether goodwill would hold.
We'd been on the road for weeks; children walking
alongside the wagons until they fell
and were thrown on top.

Last Monday, however, we made landfall. The ridge achieved
and this small place found. We pitched at the river.
The days spread out and the nerves grew softer:
perhaps they would let us stay.

Too much to hope. This morning we found the red mess of a cat,
clumped in break and blood, waiting by the fire.
We were miles off by ten, when John caught up with us,
the wet knife in his belt and the smoke rising behind him.

THAT NO PRISON WILL HOLD YOU

> *Suddenly there was a great earthquake, so that the foundations of the prison were shaken; and immediately all the doors were opened and everyone's chains were loosed. And the keeper of the prison, awaking from sleep and seeing the prison doors open, supposing the prisoners had fled, drew his sword and was about to kill himself.*
> — Acts 16: 26-27

The gaoler's boy, Simon, did not see his master

raise the knife to his own throat once the noise had died.

The rats were out through the hole in the wall before

the last brick had fallen and the full damage understood.

All night he had heard the whirling song

of the two men brought in at dusk;

the loud sound of their pleading had split to the roar

of incantation and demand. The gaoler had known them on sight

as men of danger and power, for who else could whip up a city?

Who else could silence a prison packed with men who knew no quiet?

As the howl of their ecstasy rose into the heat of the night

he had thrown Simon from the office,

shouting to *get clear* before all hell broke loose.

Afterwards the gaoler had done as they said and submitted,

that they might spare him from his charges, those men

now loosed and growling revenge.

Simon had seen none of this. He had heard the rising roar, stumbled,

fell in the passageway.

Firemen found him under the rooftiles and called it

after those men had left town.

THE CANON

Reading her message to me out loud, I was less convinced by it.
I never doubted the text was sincere, and I couldn't ignore the turns of phrase
that were unmistakably hers, when she'd made up her mind.
Something in me lessened, though, the effect of the lines in front of me,
when I spoke them back. She'd be pleased, I knew, to hear me mutter
'Nothing if not well-crafted' under my breath as I poured a drink
and laid the words on the table. The achievement of our art is bound up
in hearing the other say something that you'd thought of,
and maybe even said first, but never as well as they'd just managed.
Most experience being universal, or at least imaginable,
it is seldom the event portrayed that we've any interest in, compared to
the talent being well-applied to transmission itself.
I'll admit that there are exceptions, but even the miracles of holy men
or the massacres of their followers are not as unthinkable as we'd often wish them.
I'm probably thinking too much of us if I think this all down to trust.
The smallest inauthenticity, then, runs through the medium faster than love would,
and does so with all the grace of a snowplow with a drunk at the wheel.
If one side of this coin has us listening rapt to a great actor reading a shopping list,
the other is our not believing certain singers, even were they to give us
the words read off their passport, including the real first name.
This was why, that afternoon, my reading of 'I have felt, for a while',

or the subsequent snapshots of my terminal flaws, sounded fake when I did them,
while reading more gospel than gospels themselves, when written by her in the message.
As I sat back with the scotch and the cough that I medicate such deliveries with,
I remembered that even matching exchanges have fallen uneven, when I've given half.
His 'I love you' ringing truer to me in that Micklegate café, too late in the day,
than those same words from me, a beat later, had sounded.
And how, for matters both logistical and dispassionate,
'I want you to fuck me so fucking much' was more believable coming from her,
in the back of that car off the ring road, than when
I'd tried it to her the night before, on an exposed bed in an empty house.
It's not that one person's lying, it's that some people just say it better.

LILBURNE'S PRAYER

Oh god; guide of hand and tongue through pamphlet, pillory and prison
who walked with me from Kineton, washed me in blood all the way to Marston,
who spoke within my Elizabeth as a happy band of offspring
and never held my temper whether facing mob or king.
God that cast the fortune which would not let me leave aside
the imperfections of paradise, though you know how long I tried,
do not weigh the lives of those whom I led into the ocean
against my surviving to see their graves, to hear their last words spoken.
Oh god that still spoke to me when all others locked me away,
do not leave me at this last, but as in prison with me stay.
Pardon all the failings and, worse, those that I never tried.
Cast away my refusal. Cast away my pride.
Do not curse my wild hope that in hell I looked to build heaven,
and for what I have spoken in Mackem, Lord, may I be forgiven.

JESUS AMONG THE SCORPIONS

Skeleton kickback, sing for the desert,
while we still have these days together.
Broken spiral, half-done loveheart,
give me a sound to remember this stillness
when I am adrift in the sandstorms of men
and parched in the white of their words,
let me think of the growl in your shape,
that I know to forgive their apish ways.

Little dangerous, blueprint for death,
don't tell them I spoke with the devil.
Tell them I trusted your kind
enough to lay down among you
and sleep to the sound of your curve
and its creak in the cold of the desert at night
and the blister of its day.

Hobnail boot with a mind of your own,
tomorrow I will leave you all,
your undone strap with its spike and the catch
of your pincers, to hand myself over
to simpler beings: their questions and anger, their weapons.
Mantrap, I wish I could stay here
with you, where the violence is honest
and scorpions hear me out.

BACK OFF AGAIN

'I'm sorry that this is so late –
I've never been good
with computers,
You've always been better at
getting things done.'
Having received this from you via email
I held back
congratulations.
I've no idea what about you
you enshrine in technophobia –
what purity you clearly think
such wireless sloth imbues.
Cain picked up the rock as he found it, so,
could we not do this again.

SEPTEMBER AND OCTOBER

That's one thing I feel more and more as I get older. Let's not round up the women and children. Let's not go over the hill and fuck up the people in the next town along. Let's not do any of that ever again.
— Kingsley Amis

There was no point denying

that the unbearable summer was gone,

so violence threw us to autumn.

The hand of death moved, that day,

from a palm to specific fingertips

pressed onto sudden locations.

Its pressure rang in downtown

as a hammer, as a trumpet,

as clear as a sudden spear, and everybody heard.

We thought the matter inarguable:

the hand of death moved, that day,

and everybody heard.

I drink with you

who hated that movement.

Hated not death but that movement.

You hid in our home from that movement.

You hid in ourselves from the sound.

You waited until the palm flattened again,

and were glad that it pounded redouble,

that it pressed back. You said:

Yes, that is where death is supposed to be,

back in its palm crushing down,

the better that we might condemn it,

the better that we might mourn it,

where it is laid before our viewpoint:

its constancy in that place, its reliable, ugly shape.

You prefer slaughter familiar and,

once so catered for, will talk about death.

Those beneath the fingertips died,

as did those pounded to dust by the palm.

Few of the dead prefer their slaughter.

You, who watch the hand, remember,

when we drink together and apart:

hate the touch of that hand to any place.

Impress that hatred upon your heart.

Hate it on your journeys and hate it at your mornings,

hate it and keep our children from it:

hate the hand of death wherever it falls,

and consider what this has been.

Do not hate the hand of death only

when it suits your eye

as to what the hand of death should look like

because, on that condition,

you lower yourself with the hand

and our children should not know you.

Let our eye not set conditional: let

our argument be real.

TWO NATIVITIES 2023

From Matthew

After he'd been taken away,

and our receptionist was checking my face,

I looked over to her, where she sat between

the gaggle of officials around her, come from the state to see,

to hand her priority, ritual, care.

Their reflective clothes, their alien words

to the pregnant girl on the stair.

What glories of tribute, these,

such tales of visitation,

that she might tell the child

when he asks who his father once was.

From Luke

'We don't have passports. Why would we ever need them?'
Three hours into the conversation of the age of the sudden bride,
of whether my work had space, and the story was starting to tremble.
A note-perfect account of the London Olympics Opening Ceremony,
with some quick mistakes thrown in, and the man behind her was looking
pleased. She was looking nowhere but into her hands.
She was holding nothing but herself
and whoever swam inside her.
I counted the cost of a life
were she left to live one outside of her own.
I looked at their application for accommodation at this speed
and at the man because of whom she was learning memory.
'I can remember Brexit, Trump,' she shook '…if that isn't enough.'
What do you mean *remember*, I wondered more than asked.
At my quiet the man turned huge, and I wondered how loudly I'd scream.
And then she looked up, having found it,
and with the last of her old life released:
'I can remember the Financial Crisis.
And Obama's first inaugural.'
He began to shout. She looked past me.
She looked into and out of me.
and I saw that small victory as all that she had
to keep them warm throughout
the long walk to another country, where passports wouldn't help them,
and the weight of what would follow.

HALFWAY FROM HELL TONIGHT
'I will not be reconstructed.' ('The Sunnyside of the Street')
i.m. SM

When word of your death slid down the line, I was struck

by the tale of Joe Strummer having to look for

the bare bones of your voice, hung on the wire,

for a syllable-by-syllable cut, a necklace strung with song.

I moved it beside the story of those in the embassy basement,

threading the shredded together to clock

who the missing were, in shattered Tehran,

both being those of the kaleidoscope settling, reeling from destruction.

But now I am playing a sea-song of yours, of the dead

and the damned coming back, and so the needle drops

both on the spin, and on to you through the sack,

to turn you around or else sew it all up to bid you the sailor's farewell.

Eyes and needles sharpen, after the recoverable or gone,

but yours is now the thread through it all, heading not homewards but on.

PETER THE HERMIT

Above all, don't fool yourself, don't say
it was a dream, your ears deceived you:
don't degrade yourself with empty hopes like these.
　— 'The God Abandons Anthony', C. P. Cavafy (trans. E. Keeley and P. Sherrard)

Peter the Hermit, 1098, admonished in silence for his attempt

to escape the work of the Siege of Antioch. Henceforth a 'fallen star',

as I have read in the Chronicles.

I make do with Jeremy Corbyn's to-camera lie

that he had not called for Article 50

to be triggered immediately,

a falsehood so easily marked –

as his call was also to-camera –

that it hardly compares to the problems involved

in slipping from the camp undetected,

let alone comprehending

being caught and drawn back in silence.

It is years from the lie but my evenings, my pubs,

are filled with Peter's men

and the usual talk

of Jews and daggers, of kill all the lawyers. Their blame.

Who can easily tell the difference

between a man leaving the bar for a smoke

and one running to catch a train?

Who sees the final flame of some space-trash

and knows it apart

from a hairy star

or the end of the battle in heaven?

FINAL SUMMIT ATTEMPT

I went on, up the incline of the fight,
fastening intent to the reach of trees above,
before the push to the ridge. How long had we been climbing,
sure, but who's time to answer?
I bet you counted it from the first turnaround,
back by the pub, when Tom and Jackie
both decided that this much work just to counter a point,
then, really, they'd be better off home.
For myself, I flagged the thing later – probably
at that time of night near the first closed gate
when, despite our sense of restlessness
and your particular brand of want,
you'd shoed me off past the kiss down your neck
and turned to the darkness, where I followed.
Pressed to the whip of the pine avenues,
from the smashed-white stone of the forester's path,
I asked if you really knew where we were headed
as sticky brown twig and stale air, leaf and branch
smeared us along on the dark climb ahead.
Tumblemess, wet grass, the watching things
that marked our way up the disputed height,
turned us in how we would grab at each other
then vanish first into the skirts of the trees then back

to find the other full three rows over.

You read the wood as your father and cast

both the leaving and distance of him in the coldness

that caught half of the air between

the rapids of wind, their breaking on stars,

and the inch of still oxygen crouched in the long green,

dark green, wet green grass

that flooded our feet on the floor.

I knew something after your father, and sent

the whole of my longing out at the trees, until we broke

the line before ten and found ourselves headed out to the ridge.

It gets cold, from here I'd shouted,

as the wind hacked away at the two of us

but you in your stride and your anger – when were you going to listen?

Now the creatures were stirring themselves,

in the stalls and canopied boxes

of watching these idiots out in the night.

Foxes, quick deer, woodlice, goats,

sheep with their daubs, and coneys exchanging

cold shoulder with the hare

that is sprung at an hour like this with intent:

as we hit the ridge and the wind came

full-on broken onto our bodies,

the bestiary silhouetted in watch

looked at us go from the dark of the trees

to the climb of the fell that was watered above us.
Now we were fighting the incline, my mother,
my seventeen brothers and sunken-in sister
all of whom railed at us, laid in the heather,
and shook the mountain that bellowed beneath us.
I was away with the sweat and full bladder,
while you wound a cable of bloodred hair
out of your face so that you could climb clearly
and *one other thing, once I've been for a piss*
as I turned to scream *what* and you ducked out of sight.
For then I knew full what it meant to be caught,
as the fuss of the valley blew up to smack me,
and when you came back, catching me at the same,
you laughed in a scream at the strength of the gale.
Then higher to moss and the spittle of hawthorn –
the thicket and stab of some gorse grown violent
but who can you see, to complain, when the weather
is blasting you back to the ground and your brothers
are betting on beer-miles, whiskies and luckies,
that their wee little me will not make it above
so they've still half a chance with herself, with me gone.
After an hour the night turned to flood,
as if water'd gone out and really bulked up.
I saw you pounce as the wild dog might spring
down on all fours, and up, and back to the furnace

of what we were doing – the half-caught *and anyway*, the grabbings of
oh and as if you'd know better or *fucker* – we crawled our way
out to the third col, and wondered if really
it wasn't too late and too cold to be racking
ourselves halfway to the clouds,
but then made the mistake of seeing each other,
and if my spit and my sweat on my face
and the rain that had flattened myself to myself
hadn't sent you down, then no more
was your scarlet expression
and everything stuck to you with the water,
or all the things built out of whisky and wrath,
and everything vicious that builds in a contest,
or one of those things you forget of a lover,
and all the great things gone from our talk,
or those massive words that turn fuckers to tempest,
and each of us out for ourselves on the other,
were ever going to turn me to home.
So I went on as blind-summits beckoned
and mirage removed the idea that
what we were after would settle
once something so small as a peak were achieved.
You went on at the side of the wind,
with the skree-run and burstings of stream to your knees
as I counted a bible of shouts from you go,

lost to the craze and the chaos of wind.
Something was spiralling where the ground stopped,
but you'd never take just a first-to-the-summit
and turned with the rock in your hand and your eye
to wreck me to fellside, lay this down for good.
I lifted the point of the whole damn debate
to set to where you would stone me from sky
and we fought in a version of love that was falling
and went on past midnight, until we were shocked
at the everything summoned in such a high state
and the valleys below that were drained of ourselves
as the argument fell to the bare inch between
the silence of my emptied mouth
and the warm wet and curl of your own.
We stayed there. We never came down.

THE HELL AND HIGH

It isn't the case that the taste of white wine

and the drop of Bud Light are the same.

What is different is what I feel

in that place in front of my heart.

After years of passing the Rubicon,

I'm finally over here. With the *fucking them*

and the wearing of rings,

hands half a foot out from the hips.

We don't really talk. I'm not here to talk.

The savings? They count for little,

but as with the difference in drink so with this:

I've tuned my tongue

to economy.

THE GUILTY
Not that you lied to me, but that I no longer believe you, has shaken me.
— *Beyond Good and Evil,* Friedrich Nietzsche

Comrades, we have all known that moment when things cannot hold

and another drink is bought, or a half-forgotten film brought up.

The hand clamps onto the button; rumble resolves to a roar and

the roof of the world rips open. *The core is gone, the core of the lie.*

Now there is chaos, chaos,

chaos and terrible light. One man took a usually lethal dose

ten years ago, working elsewhere. Last year, after the core blew out,

I sent him out to see what the noise had been;

an exploded wife, perhaps, or another violent man.

He came back in, face lashed with red, barely able to speak, retching.

On top of his prior exposure I didn't see him lasting the week.

But while there was hair loss and shrieking at night

he didn't end up gone.

He lives on Shetland, now. Drinks water. Looks out of the window.

For others there has been no such life. When the effects of the lie set in

the dull routine of response enacts.

But that night, with parts of it raw on the ground

everything burned to the touch.

After a night spent fighting chaos, around the lie blown open,

who does not want to wrap the beaten body in metal,

climb into a hole and sink under cement?

Lies blow through a life in the days and weeks after their first exposure

and redden all that they touch, until it seems that

birds fall from the sky as excuses

and men scream in hospital wards as they melt from sheer discovery.

Late at night I take my drink to the table and notice a single hair

floating on the scotch. And I know

that for all that I wrapped myself in precaution,

however much composure I maintained,

something has got through to me. Damn the reports.

MISTER HANDTOTHROAT

                                        applied
for the 'Understanding of the Court':
that the multiple absconds heaped
feet-thick at his door,
totaling many thousands of pounds
and countless hours of my time,
were to do with misunderstandings
and not his track record
of theft.

The Court declined that reading and ordered
the whole lot be repaid.
This he will complete,
at the rate that he's doing it,
sometime around
the minute my grandson
forgets which name more
of the people he's facing
knew me by
as he starts the address.

For all that I hated the tracking,
the rancid desperations

of liar and lie,

for all that I'd gladly help him pay

from my own purse

if it got him out of my life

a day sooner than that day,

I've time for a man who lives up to his name

rather than split himself between two

for no reason better

than a centring of shame

that I'm an equal distance gone from, now,

that I might have to pick up a third.

At least he was caught

in his second language

while I'm still not done with my first.

APHRODITE

I am comforted by couples composed of people younger than me
who seem to be on an early date in a bookshop in the morning.
While I'm shuffling my headache round the Stationery section
they're going after laughter between Essays and Graphic Novels.
As much as it must be a neutral space, the place also offers options.
All the conversation they are likely to have is already in this building,
it's just a matter of one of them getting there before the other
reads which book said it first, and ceases to smile.
In the spirit of giving a handful of them a few more second's grace,
I move books to other shelves, where they're less likely to give it away;
though worry, as I do so, that I am upsetting some vast neural program
carefully laid out in a deal between the Fates and several publishers.
There they go, out the door, as I remove the dictionary from Erotica
and hope that this sets us all straight.

SPEECH
with Liv

You can go to too many weddings.

The father tearfully mangling his daughter

my wee baby or *my delicate flower*

with words as fully meant with love

as those of the best man's *my best mate*

and the night in Bradford that turned too much.

This being as close as they let love get

without that stare and the threat therein.

As their speeches conjure the little girl

and the drunken prick of a teenage boy

you wonder who's letting these kids get hitched

and when do we call the police?

You can leave too many wrung out at the thought of

the things that we let words do to people.

STRAIGHTSMOUTH
after Sean O'Brien

How in the name of all our dead we found ourselves in Straightsmouth,
I'm yet to understand. This was not the plan, not my plan at least.
We had set out for greenery, even the high price and polish of
a little town done good. But here we are in Straightsmouth,
with half a truck of rotting books and no buyer to relieve us.
The main street's stuck, from two miles off, with the circus of a funeral:
who let the clown in the stovepipe hat lead their mother into a ditch?
Come to think of it – might they read, as they wait for the council to lift the limo
out of the hole that it's nosing? Two dead bars and a sandwich shop,
the nail salon's dog reading Tatler in its corner,
a cinema ordered three times too large for the town that it's been dropped in.
A second-hand place all told, from the market to the surgery
where people are having the discarded parts of their neighbours stapled on.
Too many flags and sagging flesh: the chaos of a public speaker
switching from refugees to the Stones, while the copper watches
another man's daughter strain herself into sixteen.
Right on time, the hearse breaks down and they carry her out,
past the ditched family, past the closed Boots, the white-washed windows
of all this closing in. They might just burn the coffin in the fenced-off football field.

'You're not from round here, are you?' First London weekend, half my life ago.
I had to laugh. Two decades in the north of having the shit ripped out me
for sounding like some southern twat or talking al reet push like
to get down there and realise that I wasn't changing anything.
So sure I'm a white guy begging your take-a-breath indulgence
of a question of identikit. He's a Patrick but that doesn't mean that
I can bend those Irish slavers, his calming their dogs in the breakers,
from his story to my history, nor raise a glass of black and white
with anything like the Gaelic, nor could I build a conflict massive:
of blood and tongue that puts the Midlands next to Teesside
in my speaking, from my parents, from the violences about,
back to the Welsh on one side or over to the Scots; my family
backtracks to the sundered, by middle names, maidens, married,
by the taken apart that lands me growing up in Sunderland
or standing out in Durham before moving down to London.
But it all came down to those two years, from five til I were seven,
laying the trap of a voice of nothing: the neutral English accent in me,
a citizen nomad lost and a stranger to himself set
far out and alone. 'No. I'm not from round here. Thanks.'

ACKNOWLEDGMENTS

My thanks to the editors of anthologies, magazines, and websites where several of these poems have previously appeared; *Atrium*, Richard Skinner at *14 Magazine*, Fran Lock at Culture Matters, Gerry Cambridge at *The Dark Horse*, Jon Stone at *Future Karaoke*, David Cooke at *The High Window*, *The Interpreter's House*, Linda Black and Claire Crowther at *Long Poem Magazine*, *Magma* and Robert Selby at *Wild Court*, likewise thanks to Aaron Kent at Broken Sleep Books.

'Straightsmouth' was longlisted for the National Poetry Competition 2024.

Thank you to those who helped with the reading and work on these poems and most of all to John Clegg, the sagest editor and friend I could wish for. Thanks also to my family.

Thank you to Olivia Evans for things said, those past telling, and everything in between.

LAY OUT YOUR UNREST

www.ingramcontent.com/pod-product-compliance
Lightning Source LLC
Chambersburg PA
CBHW030051100426
42734CB00038B/1101